discover**more**

Transportation

Focus on Motorcycles

Doug Bradley

Britannica
Educational Publishing

IN ASSOCIATION WITH

THE ROSEN PUBLISHING GROUP

Published in 2026 by Britannica Educational Publishing (a trademark of Encyclopædia Britannica, Inc.)
in association with The Rosen Publishing Group, Inc.
2544 Clinton Street, Buffalo, NY 14224

Distributed exclusively by Rosen Publishing.
To see additional Britannica Educational Publishing titles, go to rosenpublishing.com.

Editor: Greg Roza
Book Design: Michael Flynn

Photo Credits: Cover OlegRi/Shutterstock.com; (series background) Dai Yim/Shutterstock.com; p. 4 https://commons.wikimedia.org/wiki/File:Veloc%C3%ADpedo_Roper_(1869).jpg; p. 5 Audio und werbung/Shutterstock.com; p. 6 xavier gallego morell/Shutterstock.com; p. 7 VanoVasaio/Shutterstock.com; p. 9 (top) adolf martinez soler/Shutterstock.com; p. 9 (bottom) Karolis Kavolelis/Shutterstock.com; p. 11 (top) Mikel Taboada/Shutterstock.com; p. 11 (bottom) CravenA/Shutterstock.com; p. 12 Don Pablo/Shutterstock.com; p. 13 Non Pertinente/Shutterstock.com; p. 14 (motorcycle tire) 5visual/Shutterstock.com; p. 14 (car tire) tanaphongpict/Shutterstock.com; p. 15 iChzigo/Shutterstock.com; p. 16 drcmarx/Shutterstock.com; p. 17 Leo Kydon/Shutterstock.com; p. 18 Everyonephoto Studio/Shutterstock.com; p. 19 Suvorov_Alex/Shutterstock.com; p. 20 Artur Didyk/Shutterstock.com; p. 21 udeyismail/Shutterstock.com; p. 23 (top) streetphotog66/Shutterstock.com; p. 23 (bottom) Parilov/Shutterstock.com; p. 24 n_defender/Shutterstock.com; p. 25 Daxiao Productions/Shutterstock.com; p. 26 Alexandr Zimovskoy/Shutterstock.com; p. 27 Nalidsa/Shutterstock.com; p. 28 Virrage Images/Shutterstock.com; p. 29 BAZA Production/Shutterstock.com.

Cataloging-in-Publication Data

Names: Bradley, Doug, 1971-.
Title: Focus on motorcycles / Doug Bradley.
Description: New York : Britannica Educational Publishing, in association with Rosen Educational Services, 2026. | Series: Discover more: transportation | Includes glossary and index.
Identifiers: ISBN 9781641905459 (library bound) | ISBN 9781641905442 (pbk) | ISBN 9781641905466 (ebook)
Subjects: LCSH: Motorcycles--Juvenile literature.
Classification: LCC TL440.15 B697 2026 | DDC 629.2275--dc23

Manufactured in the United States of America

Some of the images in this book illustrate individuals who are models. The depictions do not imply actual situations or events.

CPSIA Compliance Information: Batch #CWBRIT26. For further information contact Rosen Publishing at 1-800-237-9932.

Contents

Life on Two Wheels 4
Who Invented the Motorcycle? 6
Why Ride a Motorcycle? 10
Making a Motorcycle 12
Let's Go! 16
Kinds of Rides. 18
Motorcycle Uses 22
Safety Measures 24
Best Bikes. 26
Get Out on the Highway! 28
Glossary 30
For More Information 31
Index 32

Life on Two Wheels

A motorcycle is a **vehicle** that has two wheels and an engine. They are used as transportation around the world. People also ride them in races or just for fun.

Motorcycles are bigger, heavier, and much faster than bicycles, but they have many similar parts. Like bicycles, motorcycles are often called bikes. Both usually have two wheels, although some motorcycles have three. Both have two handlebars and a central body with a seat. Both can be balanced to stand upright by the rider with the simple act of putting both feet on the ground.

The first motorcycles were bicycles with an engine added.

One reason people love motorcycles is because they enjoy being outside on a nice day.

There are many kinds of motorcycles, but they all have one thing in common that makes them different from bicycles: an engine. An engine gives the motored bike speed. It is the reason motorcycles are faster than bicycles. However, the smaller size of motorcycle engines makes most motorcycles slower than the fastest cars.

WORD WISE

VEHICLES ARE THINGS USED TO TRANSPORT PEOPLE OR GOODS. THIS COULD BE A MOTORCYCLE, AN AUTOMOBILE, A SEMI TRUCK, AND AIRPLANE, AND MORE.

Who Invented the Motorcycle?

Bicycles have been around since the early 1800s. The first bicycles were very simple, but inventors kept adding new parts, such as pedals, to improve riders' experiences. Some people also wanted to find a way to make bicycles go faster.

In the mid-1800s people began experimenting with using engines to make cars. Some of those people started by adding motors to bicycles. In 1884 English inventor Edward Butler attached a simple motor to a tricycle. His machine had two wheels in front and one in back. The rider sat between the two front wheels.

An early popular form of bicycle was the penny-farthing. It had one giant wheel and one small wheel. They were fast, but hard to control.

The first motorcycle Daimler made is now displayed in the Mercedes Museum in Stuttgart, Germany.

Gottlieb Daimler, a German engineer, is usually credited with inventing the motorcycle in 1885. Daimler added a small **internal-combustion engine** to a bicycle. This engine finally allowed the rider to move forward on two wheels without pedaling. Daimler also built one of the first gas-powered automobiles.

WORD WISE

AN INTERNAL-COMBUSTION ENGINE CREATES POWER BY BURNING FUEL INSIDE THE ENGINE.

Over the years, motorcycle design changed drastically. The rides have become smoother and faster. Motorized bikes became popular during World War I (1914–18). They were used to deliver messages and supplies to soldiers on faraway battlefields. They could travel over rough lands. They also used less fuel than cars and trucks.

Some early motorcycle manufacturers built thousands of bikes for military use. The American company Harley-Davidson and Triumph in Great Britain were two of these companies. Harley made nearly 20,000 motorcycles for the U.S. military during the war.

After the war, motorcycle use soared. Harley became the biggest motorcycle manufacturer in the world. The company sold more than 28,000 motorcycles in 67 countries in 1920. Demand rose and fell slightly over the years, but Harley alone produced 90,000 motorcycles for use in World War II (1939–45). Motorcycle use rose greatly after that.

By World War I, the modern motorcycle was beginning to take shape.

compare and contrast

Why do you think the motorcycle became more popular during the World Wars? They were cheaper to make, for one. Can you think of any other reasons?

After World War 2, many servicepeople who fought in the war purchased Harley-Davidson motorcycles that had been used in battle but were restored.

Why Ride a Motorcycle?

Why do people enjoy driving motorcycles? Many people ride motorcycles because they enjoy the ability to travel fast alone. They can see the sights on their open ride, feel the vibration of the engine, and experience the wind in their hair. Some people use their motorcycles to get around their own city. Others take their bikes on long trips across the country.

Not all motorcycle riding is done alone. Some bikes have room for a passenger to sit behind the driver. Other motorcycles have a sidecar to carry another person. A sidecar has one wheel and usually a small trunk to carry things in the rear.

Motorcycles are smaller and, therefore, cheaper to buy than most cars. Still, today's big bikes are expensive to buy and care for. Luckily, they use much less gasoline than cars do, making them more affordable to drivers.

Many motorcycles have room for a passenger in addition to the driver.

compare and contrast

If you were in need of a new vehicle, would you get a car or a motorcycle? Why?

The price of a motorcycle depends on the brand, how powerful the engine is, and how many "extras" you get with the motorcycle (mostly items that improve the performance of the vehicle).

Making a Motorcycle

Like bicycles, motorcycles have two tires, a seat, handlebars, and a sturdy steel frame that holds the bike together. However, that's where the similarities end.

Motorcycles usually get power from gasoline that feeds the engine. The handlebars on a motorcycle have controls for the throttle, clutch, and front brake. The throttle affects the speed of the bike by controlling how much air can flow to the engine. The air is needed to mix with gasoline so the bike gets energy to move.

What's the biggest difference between bikes and motorcycles? It's the engine of course!

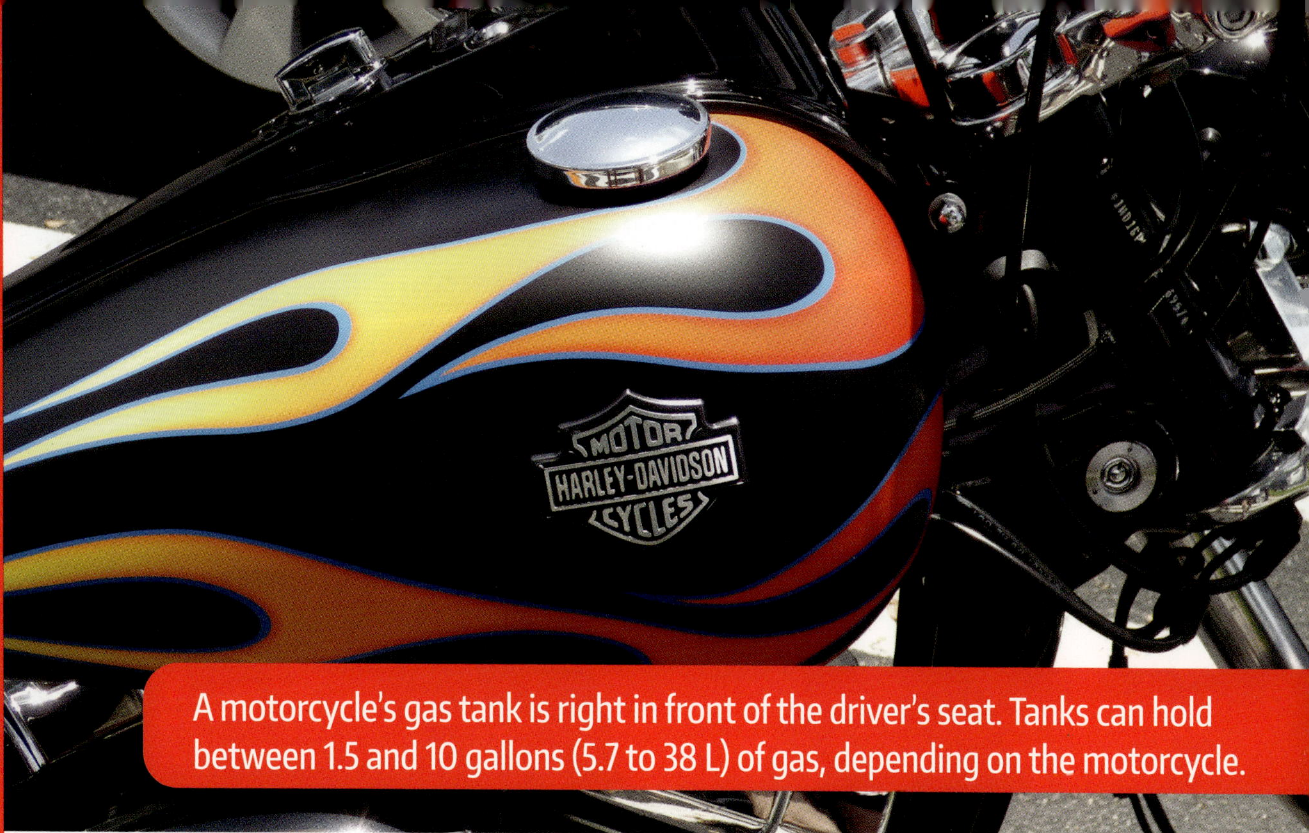

A motorcycle's gas tank is right in front of the driver's seat. Tanks can hold between 1.5 and 10 gallons (5.7 to 38 L) of gas, depending on the motorcycle.

The brake control on the handlebars is connected to the front wheel (a foot pedal controls the rear brake). Putting pressure on it allows the wheel to slow and stop. The clutch control allows the rider to change gears. Higher gears allow a motorcycle to go faster and lower gears help a motorcycle climb hills easier.

Consider This

Which type of vehicle do you think uses more gas per mile (km), a motorcycle or a car? Why do you think that?

Most motorcycles are driven on streets and highways just like cars. Some types, however, are used on dirt paths and even open land. Both kinds have **sturdy** tires to allow the bike to move easily and quickly over many types of land.

A motorcycle's tires are much narrower than a car's tires.

Filling up at the pump will cost less for motorcycle drivers than car drivers.

Motorcycle tires are more rounded than car tires. This helps when turning corners since a motorcycle leans to the side as it is turning. The front wheel of a motorcycle is connected to the handlebars. This wheel is used by the rider to guide the bike—forward, backward, and in turns.

The rear wheel is connected to the engine by a chain or a belt. The engine is the power source for the bike. Most motorcycles are powered by combustion engines.

WORD WISE

STURDY MEANS FIRMLY BUILT OR PUT TOGETHER. MOTORCYCLE TRIES NEED TO BE STURY TO HOLD UP OVER HUNDREDS OF MILES.

Let's Go!

Motorcycle engines are very similar to car engines. Electricity powers some, but most use gasoline or a mixture of oil and gasoline. Gasoline gets hot and burns inside the engine. The engine is called a combustible engine because little explosions, or combustions, are what power the bike.

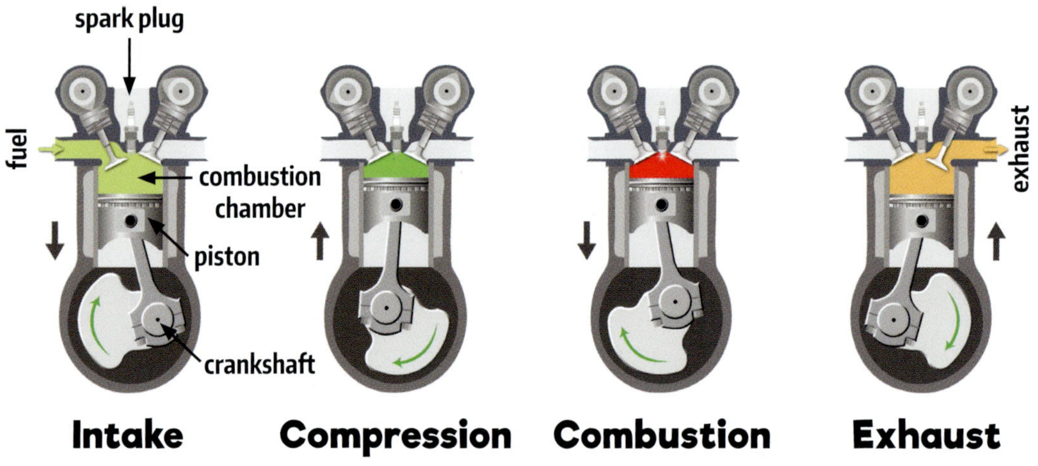

This shows the four-stroke engine cycle. These four steps happen over and over very quickly.

Some motorcycles have a V-twin engine. This means that the pistons are at an angle to each other, making a V shape.

Most engines are made up of pistons, a cylinder block (with up to six tubelike cylinders), and a head in front. The pistons are parts that move up and down in the cylinder block. The movement is made when fuel (gasoline) and air mix. This causes sparks that light up in mini explosions. Valves open and close to allow the fuel and air mixture to enter the combustion chamber. The moving pistons turn a part called a crankshaft. It transforms, or changes, the energy from the pistons. This force is sent to the rear wheel of the motorcycle. This is what moves the motorcycle forward.

Consider This

The parts covering motorcycle pistons have thin gaps between strips of metal called fins. These help to cool down the engine. How do you think that works?

Kinds of Rides

When selecting a motorcycle, it's important to think about how it will be used. For example, riding on paved roads is very different from riding on soft dirt, sand, or rocky areas. That's one of the reasons there are so many kinds of motorcycles.

Large touring bikes provide drivers with a comfortable ride.

Three-wheel motorcycles are easier to drive, have more room for passengers, and can have larger engines.

Motorcycles include street bikes, cruisers, touring bikes, racing bikes, trail bikes, and small scooters. Street bikes are used on paved roads. They include headlights, license plates, horns, and turn signals just like cars. One type of street bike, called a cruiser, has a low seat and higher handlebars. The cruiser is for casual riders. Some motorcycle, called trikes, have three wheels!

Consider This

Some motorcycle tires are rounded with deep treads, while others have rows of raised rubber. Which do you think is used for street bikes, and which is used for trail bikes?

Large touring bikes have a windshield and padded seats. They also have space in back or on the sides to carry luggage. Some even have a sidecar storage unit on one side. These bikes are used by riders who enjoy long motorcycle trips on highways.

Some motorcycles are small and light. They tend to be less expensive and are better for riding on rough surfaces. Larger, heavier motorcycles are hard to steer over rocky surfaces. Dirt, trail, or off-road motorcycles are small and do not have the equipment, like headlights and turn signals, that are needed for travel on paved roads. They are built for speed and quick handling. The rider usually sits high up and leans forward on these bikes.

Dirt bikes are made to handle rough, uneven racecourses.

In some countries, such as Vietnam, shown here, scooters are a far better way of getting around congested city streets.

Small street bikes include scooters and **mopeds**. They are lighter than standard street bikes and do not have as much power. However, they are cheaper to buy, use less gasoline, and can easily move through traffic. This is why they are very popular on the roads of some crowded parts of the world, especially in Asia and Europe.

WORD WISE

A MOPED IS A SMALL, LIGHT MOTORCYCLE THAT CAN ALSO BE PEDALED LIKE A BICYCLE.

Motorcycle Uses

Many people use a motorcycle for everyday travel. Some jobs depend on the use of a motorcycle. Police officers drive motorcycles as one way to patrol roads. The military still uses bikes as well.

Motorcycle racing is a popular sport in many parts of the world. There are many different kinds of races. Some take place on paved tracks or on dirt tracks. One of the most popular forms is called motocross. Motocross started in France and was brought to the United States in the 1960s. People of all ages compete in different levels of the sport. The riders race over rough ground. They make many turns and go up and down steep hills. They drive through muddy patches and jump over bumps and other obstacles. Riders wear special clothing to protect themselves while racing.

Motorcycle cops can often get to scenes quicker than police cars.

compare**and**contrast

What are some similarities between police motorcycles and motocross motorcycles? What are some differences?

Like all motorcyclists, motocross racers should wear a helmet. However, they also wear other forms of protection, such as thick boots, heavy gloves, and padding.

Safety Measures

Motorcycles are far more dangerous to drive than cars. That's because there are fewer kinds of protection for drivers and passengers. There is no roof or metal on the sides to protect people in accidents. Most motorcycles do not have seatbelts or airbags that protect riders in a crash.

Helmets are important. But a helmet with a visor will protect a rider's eyes from things in the air, such as bugs, rocks kicked up by other vehicles, and precipitation.

Many motorcycle riders wear leather jackets and pants. They may look cool, but leather also helps protect a rider in case of a fall.

This is why helmets are so important. They protect the rider's head and also keep bugs and other distractions away. Motorcycle helmets sometimes include a clear panel in front that protects the face. Boots, gloves, and heavy clothing (sometimes leather) also protect riders.

A special motorcycle license is needed to drive on roads. People who want to get a license must pass written and driving tests. In many places, people have to pass both the motorcycle and the automobile driver's license tests so that they can drive with cars on the road.

Consider This

Only 18 states have made it illegal to ride a motorcycle without a helmet. Twenty-nine states have exemptions (ways out of) helmet use (mostly related to age). Only 3 states have no laws regarding motorcycle helmets. Which do you think is the best law?

Best Bikes

There are many motorcycle manufacturers in the world, but some of them have a huge following. They include Harley-Davidson, Ducati, Honda, and BMW. Honda is a Japanese company that also makes cars. BMW, a German company, also makes cars. Harley and Ducati only make motorcycles. Harley is an American company that has been in business since the 1910s. Italy's Ducati is owned by the German automobile company Audi. Ducati has been making bikes since 1946.

Harley-Davidson is an American motorcycle company founded in 1903. They've sold many popular models over the years.

Honda makes all kinds of motorcycles—cruisers, high-speed racing bikes, scooters, and more.

In the United States, Harley-Davidson is the most popular motorcycle manufacturer. Honda sells the most in the world, with more than 20 million bikes sold in 2024. A large number of these bikes were scooters and smaller models sold mainly in India, China, and other parts of Asia. Approximately four out of ten motorcycles in the world are Hondas.

Consider This

Motorcycle companies such as Harley-Davidson use bike parts made in other parts of the word and assemble them in the United States. Why might a motorcycle company do that?

Get Out on the Highway!

The motorcycle has been a popular mode of transportation and sport for over 120 years! People have been riding motorcycles in different forms for that long. The popularity of motorcycles continues to grow around the world. They appeal to many people because they are a relatively inexpensive, easy way to get around.

Some motorcycle riders don't necessarily have somewhere to go. Riding is enough of a reason to get out on the open road!

Not every motorcycle rider wants to speed along lonely highways. Some prefer to scoot around city centers or scenic areas!

There are always new bike styles being made to improve on design, speed, and comfort. Safety is also a major concern. New ideas for helmets, safety gear, and even seatbelts are being developed. Many bike makers are also trying to make motorcycles that more people can afford to buy.

People who love motorcycles enjoy their ease of use and the feel of the wind in their hair. They often ride together with other fans of motorcycles. They may join one of the many clubs for motorcycle riders. The American Motorcyclist Association oversees racing events and promotes the use of motorcycles throughout the country.

Consider This

Now that you've learned all about motorcycles, do you think you'd like to drive one some day? Why or why not? What kind of motorcycle do you see yourself riding?

Glossary

assemble To put together.

brake A device for slowing or stopping movement.

clutch The part on the handlebars of a motorcycle that disengages power between the engine and transmission so the driver can change gears.

device A piece of equipment that serves a special purpose.

distraction Something that makes it hard to pay attention.

engine A machine that changes energy, such as heat from burning fuel, into mechanical motion.

gasoline A liquid that comes from natural gas and petroleum and is used especially as a fuel for engines.

grooves Long, narrow channels in the surface of an object.

handlebar A bar with a handle at each end, used for steering a bicycle or a motorcycle.

manufacturers Companies that employ people to make things.

paved Covered with material, such as stone or concrete, that forms a firm and level surface for travel.

pedals Levers (such as on a piano, bike, or sewing machine) worked by the foot.

pistons Sliding pieces moved by or moving against the pressure of a fluid (such as steam or hot gases). A piston usually consists of a short, solid cylinder moving within a larger hollow cylinder.

popular Commonly liked or approved.

sidecar A car attached to the side of a motorcycle for a passenger.

throttle The part on the handlebars of a motorcycle that enables the driver to affect how much air mixes with gasoline to give the motorcycle energy to work.

traffic The vehicles and people moving along a route.

trunk The enclosed space usually in the rear of an automobile for carrying things.

valves Mechanical devices by which the flow of liquid, gas, or other loose material may be controlled by movable parts.

For More Information

Books

Gunzi, Christiane. *Motorcycles*. New York, NY: Gareth Stevens, 2024.

Latham, Bethany. *Motorcycles*. Mendota Heights, MN: North Star Editions, 2026.

Websites

American Motorcyclist Association
americanmotorcyclist.com
Do you have any questions remaining about motorcycles in the United States? You will find all the answers here!

Harley-Davidson History
auto.howstuffworks.com/harley-davidson-history.htm
Learn all about the history of the Harley-Davidson motorcycle company at Howstuffworks.

Publisher's note to educators and parents: Our editors have carefully reviewed these websites to ensure that they are suitable for students. Many websites change frequently, however, and we cannot guarantee that a site's future contents will continue to meet our high standards of quality and educational value. Be advised that students should be closely supervised whenever they access the internet.

Index

B

brakes, 12, 13
Butler, Edward, 6

C

clutch, 12, 13
crankshaft, 17

D

Daimler, Gottlieb, 7

E

engine, 4, 5, 6, 7, 10, 11, 12, 15, 16, 17, 19

G

gasoline, 10, 12, 13, 16, 17, 21

H

handlebars, 4, 12, 13, 15, 19
Harley-Davidson, 8, 9, 26, 27
Honda, 26, 27

K

kinds of motorcycles, 18, 19, 20, 21

M

military, 8, 9, 22
motorcycle license, 25

P

passenger, 10, 11, 19, 24
pistons, 17

R

racing, 19, 22, 23, 27, 29

S

safety, 24, 25, 29
seat, 4, 12, 13, 19, 20

T

throttle, 12
tires/wheels, 4, 6, 12, 13, 14, 15, 17, 19